The HOPE HANDBOOK FOR CHRISTIANS

POWERFUL, INSPIRATIONAL, HOPEFUL TWEETS THAT ENCOURAGE MOTIVATE, AND SPEAK TO YOUR SPIRIT

THE SEARCH FOR PERSONAL GROWTH

GERMANY KENT

The Hope Handbook for Christians

Copyright @2015 by Germany Kent

Visit us online at www.TheHopeHandbook.com

ISBN: 978-0-9961468-1-4 (ebook)
ISBN: 978-0-9961468-2-1

Library of Congress Control Number: 2015904482

Compiled by Germany Kent

Published by: Star Stone Press, 10736 Jefferson Blvd #164, Culver City, CA 90230

Printed in the United States of America

Amongst inspirational tweets of hope compiled using wise words from my grandmother, original content, and tweets of knowledge from other tweeters, you will find words of hope passed along from many other wise people who have crossed my path on my journey to self-discovery. You will also find motivational messages as spoken or written by world leaders and motivational gurus.

Books are available in quantity for promotional or premium use. Requests for information should be addressed to: Star Stone Press, 10736 Jefferson Blvd #164, Culver City, CA 90230, for information and discounts and terms. You may also send a request at www.GermanyKent.com

CONTENTS

INTRODUCTION 1
PART ONE - SEEK GOD FIRST 5
PART TWO - TRUST IN THE POWER OF PRAYER 83
PART THREE - STAY HUMBLE 159
PART FOUR - SOAR HIGH WITH FAITH AND TRUST 239
AFTER THOUGHTS FROM THE AUTHOR 321
ABOUT THE AUTHOR 322
TO OUR READERS 324

REFLECTIONS
MEDITATIONS
INSPIRATIONS

"No eye has seen, no ear has heard, and no mind has imagined what God has prepared for those who love him."
- 1 Corinthians 2:9

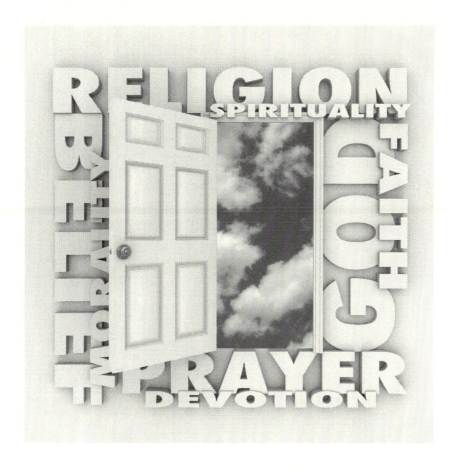

INTRODUCTION

Christianity has more active users than Twitter. With one billion followers, it is the most major religious and belief form of the world. As Christians, we believe in God and His teachings as referred to in the Holy Bible. Most of us believe salvation is gained by those who have faith, and by showing humility toward God.

God created each of us with unique gifts, talents, and personalities, and has shaped our lives and fixed it so we can put them to use. You must learn to trust God's timing because He will put it all together for you. God will not give you more than you can handle.

The depth you are willing to allow God to take you is in direct proportion to the height He will elevate you. What God has for you is better than anything you could plan for yourself. Make plans; but trust God to upgrade them.

If you have a big challenge today, that means you have a big destiny. When times are hard, God is testing you to see how strong you are. Everything that you are going through is preparing you for what you have prayed for. Your angels will safely guide and support you through this change.

Never doubt yourself, and always remember that God created you divinely perfect for your life purpose. God will challenge you to help you grow. God is getting you ready for greater levels of blessings.

Being a Christian is more than a personal and transforming relationship with God. It is also a public and transforming relationship with the world. As Christians we believe in brotherly love, which is emphasized in acts of charity, kindness, and forgiveness. In addition, Jesus' teachings insist on justice and mercy toward all people.

You can increase or decrease the amount of joy that you radiate, so place your attention on showering huge amounts of bliss wherever you go. Make your spiritual walk with God your life essence.

God did not save us by grace so that we may live in disgrace. You are where God wants you to be at this very moment. Every experience is part of his divine plan.

My prayers are with you for health, peace, and happiness for you and your loved ones. Realize how blessed you are and let his light shine through you.

God bless you all!

PART ONE
SEEK GOD FIRST

"But seek ye first the kingdom of God, and his righteousness; and all these things shall be added unto you."

– Matthew 6:33

🐦 Love one another.

🐦 Seek God first and he will give you everything you need.

🕊 The world doesn't need a new definition for Christianity; it needs a new demonstration of it.

🕊 God's timing is always right.

- God's grace is not gender based, has nothing to do with politics, or social status.

- God's grace is beyond divisions.

🕊 God is preparing the right people, the right circumstances, and the right breaks for your future. When it's your time you will feel like you just walked into God's blessings.

🕊 It won't be about God if we make everything about us.

- Develop a tremendous faith in God and that will give you a humble yet soundly realistic faith in yourself

- Live your life in a way that is pleasing to God.

🕊 It's better to please God and have some people upset with you, then to please people and have God upset with you.

🕊 If it keeps you from becoming closer to God, it doesn't deserve to be part of your life.

🐦 Peace on the outside comes from knowing God on the inside.

🐦 Blessed if you do, blessed if you don't, blessed no matter what.

- Faith knows no limits and neither should you.

- Chasing your purpose means ignoring the criticism of others, and trusting in God's ultimate plan for your life.

🕊 Refuse to be fearful about what will happen to you. God is faithful and He will take care of you if you trust Him.

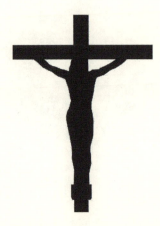

🕊 Never let people's negative thoughts about you hinder you from accomplishing what God put in your heart.

- Following God isn't glamorous, but it is so beautiful. Your hands will get dirty and your heart will get wrecked, but love makes it worth it.

- Peace on the outside comes from knowing God on the inside.

🕊 God turns broken pieces into masterpieces.

🕊 Whatever God is urging you to clear away cannot begin to be compared to what He ultimately wants to bring you.

🕊 Don't worry if people don't understand you, you have almighty God's approval.

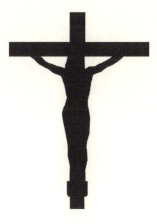

🕊 Don't give up on what God has called you to do. The end result is worth the pain.

- Thank God for your life today; for your health, your family, or your home. Many people don't have these things.

- If you keep replaying your hurts and bad breaks, you are never going to heal. It's time to change the channel and think positive.

🐦 We are to be radiant, grateful, buoyant people basking in our blessings and striving cheerfully toward our dreams.

🐦 Never apologize for being a Christian.

- Until God's love and acceptance is enough, nothing else will do.

- Every time you meet needs in Jesus' name, you build the kingdom and become God's hand.

🕊 There is unity in the body of Christ.

🕊 To fear God is to believe God. To believe God is to obey Him.

🕊 The plan of God for your life is utterly beyond your ability, but you will surely succeed if you depend on His grace.

🕊 Have patience; God is not finished yet.

🕊 Humility opens the door to God's best for our lives.

🕊 Our willingness to forgive is one of the greatest evidences of Christ within us.

- Sin will take you farther than you want to go, keep you longer than you want to stay, and cost you more than you want to pay.

- Forgive others as God forgave you.

- You are beautiful. Don't allow anyone to tell you less. God made you.

- God does not dwell in an unclean temple.

🕊 Believe God for what some say is impossible.

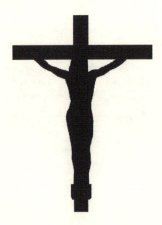

🕊 We serve a God who specializes in impossibilities.

🕊 Seek God's voice. Some things God only wants to tell you.

🕊 For God hath not given us the spirit of fear; but of power, and of love and a sound mind.

- The downfall of any individual is vanity, pride, and idolatry. Don't let arrogance cause you to forfeit your place in the kingdom of God.

- Have faith. Give generously. Spread hope. Laugh frequently. Love unconditionally. Live fully.

🕊 If our God is for us who can be against us?

🕊 God's word has full authority.

🐦 God is waiting on you to accept Him.

🐦 God will never leave you; regardless of how many times you run away from Him. You can't escape His love for you. It has no bounds.

- Living as a Christian and a Leader is challenging, but we are called to where we are, to live passionately, and honestly with love.

- Your inner glow comes from the light of God, and your light can never be extinguished or soiled. You are eternally bright and beautiful.

🕊 Do your best and leave the results to God. -Norman Vincent Peale

🕊 God didn't bring you this far to abandon you.

🕊 Everything is working in your favor and for your benefit.

🕊 Maybe you never fit in with the world because God created you to stand out for Him.

🕊 Through the good and the bad, know that God is always with you.

🕊 Life is very short, so forgive quickly, believe slowly, love truly, laugh loudly and always remember to thank God for it all.

🕊 Live a life with purpose.

🕊 Until we replace the facts of our circumstances with the truth of God's Word, things are never going to change.

- Jesus simply said, follow me.

- Don't ask God to guide your footsteps if you're not willing to move your feet.

🕊 Three things God will NEVER do; fail you, abandon you, or give up on you.

🕊 You are a blessing to the world.

- Everything you ever needed to find joy and purpose in this life can be found in Jesus. Call on Him. Seek Him out.

- Every life is worth saving in God's eyes.

🐦 Never doubt yourself, and always remember that God created you divinely perfect for your life purpose.

🐦 You can help others awaken their spiritual endowments and inspire them to hold a more positive outlook.

🕊 Have faith that God is living out a divine plan through you.

🕊 Don't magnify your problem; magnify your God.

- God is for you; even when it seems like circumstances are against you. Wait it out.

- Thank God, for opening the doors that need to be opened and for closing the doors that need to be closed.

🕊 You were uniquely planned, created and molded for such a time as this.

🕊 You are a beautiful and powerful reflection of divinity.

🐦 The bigger your life purpose, the more your ego tries to distract you, and bring down your courage. Stay strong and focused on your spiritual path.

🐦 Life in the Spirit produces living fruit. And this fruit has in it the seed for still more fruit.

🕊 Go after your dream, no matter how unattainable others think it is.

🕊 Smile. You are six feet above.

- God can only take control when you are willing to lose control. You will have authority in your command when you are submitted to His.

- The greatest obstacle in your life now is really your greatest opportunity to see God work a miracle.

🕊 You are not forgotten. Humble yourselves under his mighty hand by casting all your cares on Him because he cares for you.

🕊 Remember to magnify God and minimize your problems today.

🕊 One of the best gifts we can give ourselves is time alone with God.

🕊 Instead of fearing dark circumstances, know that you are eternally safe and protected.

🕊 The closer we get to God, the harder the enemy attacks.

🕊 Bad company corrupts good character.

🐦 With God, devastation can turn into revelation.

🐦 You can't live the Christian life without a band of Christian friends, without a family of believers in which you find a place.

🐦 By God's amazing grace we have been saved from the depravity of sin & raised together in Christ!

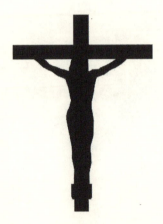

🐦 Sometimes you have to get knocked down lower than you've ever been, to stand up taller than you than you ever were.

- Declare God's will with purpose and empowerment.

- As you step into the battle for truth, God will supply all you need, and your faith will grow ever stronger in Him.

- Say this: "Dear angels, please give me the courage and motivation to take action as you have guided me."

- Surrender and release to the God whatever is worrying or bothering you, and He will take care of it accordingly.

- God is a mighty and powerful essence of all-encompassing love. This love is so bright that it deflects all darkness.

- Remember, God welcomes your continual requests for His assistance, so don't ever worry about overwhelming Him.

🕊 God doesn't give you the people you want, he gives you the people you need.

🕊 God is our refuge and strength, a very present help in trouble.

- We are to shine brightly in this dark world and lead many to righteousness.

- Discipleship is relational, intentional, and transformational.

- God won't always give you what you think you want, because He'd rather give you what He knows you need instead.

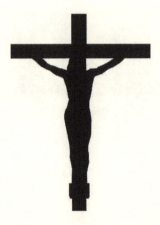

- God is moving in every situation in your life for His Glory. All things are working together for your good.

🐦 Don't follow the crowd. Follow Jesus.

🐦 Those who call themselves followers of Jesus must love those who others see as un-loveable.

🕊 When the storm and winds come, they will expose your foundation.

🕊 Grace empowers you to live from a place of victory.

🐦 Blessed if you do, blessed if you don't, blessed no matter what.

🐦 Don't tell God how to help; just ask for what you want.

🕊 Faith is the little voice in your heart that whispers Yes when the world around you is saying no.

🕊 Although you may not feel their presence at the time, your guardian angels are even closer to you during your toughest moments.

- 🐦 The very first thing we should do when we come before God's presence is to thank Him.

- 🐦 Discover God's wonderful grace.

🐦 God + anyone = unlimited potential.

🐦 God says you're wonderfully made - anything less than that is a false identity.

🕊 If God can give through you, He will give to you.

🕊 From start to finish, God has worked everything out in our favor.

🕊 You will never reach a point where you have nothing to give.

🕊 Give any cares and worries to heaven right now.

- Invite grace to join you on your day and watch how much easier your day can flow, even when obstacles appear before you.

- You cannot microwave a disciple. Discipleship is a crock pot recipe. It is a long slow process.

- 🐦 Any view other than God's view is a distorted reality.

- 🐦 Give thanks in the midst of disappointment.

- Your past is a place of reference, not a place of residence.

- Worry, fear, stress, and anxiety seem more natural than thanksgiving. But, thanksgiving is the cure for worry and fear.

- Clearly not everything that happens to us is good. But God is at work in every circumstance that we face.

- God is love. God is strength. God is courage. God is comfort.

🕊 Doing what God has called you to do is what makes you successful.

🕊 God has demonstrated his faithfulness in the past. He will demonstrate his faithfulness now.

- Be still and let God work. Allow Him to do everything He has always wanted to do in your life today.

- Praise God even when you don't understand what He's doing.

🕊 In the days to come you will testify of your breakthroughs and miracles.

🕊 God will never ask you to do what He has not wired and equipped you to do.

🐦 It really doesn't matter what others think of you, as your spiritual truth can't be changed by anyone's opinion.

🐦 God cannot and will not fail you.

🐦 God takes what the enemy has meant for bad and turns it for your good.

🐦 What seems to be a problem or block is often really a blessing in disguise.

- Breathe and thank God for giving you life.

- That obstacle that looks permanent is really only temporary. God is saying, "If you'll stay in faith, I will deliver you from this."

🐦 Let go of the disappointments and setbacks in your life and hang on to the promises of God for your future.

🐦 Life can be hard, but the arms of God are strong enough to carry you through the difficult times.

🕊 God's more interested in where we're heading with Him than all the places we've gone alone.

🕊 If you want to change your life, ask God to let you see yourself and others thru His eyes.

🕊 God can turn your wounds into wisdom and your pain into purpose.

🕊 God's grace knows no boundaries.

- Speak death to every relationship, friendship that is not pleasing to God.

- Remind yourself daily that God is working for your good even if you don't understand what's going on.

🕊 God can help you overcome any trial.

🕊 It may not be easy, you may not understand it, but faith is trusting God when life doesn't make sense.

- You sin? God forgives. You worry? God is in control. You're empty? God restores. You're alone? God is with you.

- Demonstrate the love of God to everyone you encounter.

🐦 Jesus is the light of the world. Let His light shine through you.

PART TWO
TRUST IN THE POWER OF PRAYER

"Therefore I say to you, whatever things you ask when you pray, believe that you receive them, and you will have them."

– Mark 11:24

🐦 There's no place like hope.

🐦 Pray for peace.

🕊 You create a season of success every time you obey an instruction from God.

🕊 If you really want to defend what you believe, live it.

- You need to start talking victory when you are staring at defeat.

- Waiting in prayer is a disciplined refusal to act before God acts.

🐦 That longing deep within reminds you that you were created for so much more than what you have seen.

🐦 Prayer changes everything because it releases God's wisdom into your circumstances.

- Spending time with God puts everything else in perspective

- When you take time with God and listen to His voice, He renews your strength and enables you to handle life.

🕊 Worship is the strategy by which we interrupt our preoccupation with ourselves and attend to the presence of God.

🕊 Your private prayers are about to be answered.

- If you never endure great burdens you can't handle great success.

- If He brought you this far, God can get you from where you are to where you ought to be.

🕊 What you lost was painful, but what you have left is powerful. He's God of what's left.

🕊 Keep the faith that your prayers are being answered.

🕊 When you bring your not enough to God's more than enough miracles happen.

🕊 If prayer isn't necessary to accomplish your plans, you aren't thinking big enough.

🕊 Prayer should be your first response, not a last resort.

🕊 Amazing grace: How sweet the sound.

🕊 Do not face the day until you've faced God in prayer.

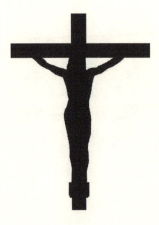

🕊 When you pray, but don't listen to God, it is a one way conversation.

🕊 Pray daily. Pray because God hears you.

🕊 God sees and hears you. He wants to move in your life.

🕊 Pray like it matters. Live like God is able to answer.

🕊 God will meet you where you are, and He has a plan just for you.

🕊 When you're in a fight, don't lose focus. Distractions have one duty: To detour, derail and cause you to doubt your destiny.

🕊 To know God is to love God. To love Him is to serve Him. To serve Him is to know Him better. To know Him better is to love Him more.

🕊 Prayer changes things.

🕊 With God nothing "just happens." Coincidence is what takes place when He decides to remain anonymous.

🕊 Fasting is a short season that produces long-term results.

🕊 Stop thinking God will use anybody but you, or bless others more than you. He believes in you more than you believe in yourself.

- It takes courage to say no to the things or people that are pulling you away from what God requires of you.

- Someone that has the favor of God has something better than silver or gold.

🕊 God knows the burdens you carry and the tears you shed. He is the healer of broken hearts, broken dreams, and broken lives. He never fails.

🕊 With God's power working in us, God can do much more than anything we can ask or imagine.

🕊 Prayer, in its most basic form, is the surging of the human spirit in its weakness, grasping at the Spirit of God in His strength.

🕊 Remember that your hope does not rest in your ability to cling to Him but in His power to hold onto you

- Keep praying, keep hoping, and keep believing. Even when it seems nothing is happening, God is moving on your behalf.

- Often times a breakdown will happen right before your breakthrough.

- Break free from the burden of grudges and pray for the one who wronged you.

- Live simply, love generously, speak truthfully and pray daily.

🕊 Untested faith is no faith at all.

🕊 Fasting is renouncing the natural to invoke the supernatural.

🕊 God takes the worst thing, throws a few of His own ingredients in there and it turns out to be a miracle. All you have to do is give it to Him.

🕊 God is still good even when things are not.

🕊 Pray the hardest when it's the hardest to pray.

🕊 Pray it out. This season will pass.

🕊 Our humility is a prerequisite for our promotion.

🕊 God is never late; we're just impatient.

- We all go through difficulty, but that challenge is not there to stop you; it's there to develop you.

- Grace is God's willingness to use His power on our behalf even though we don't deserve it.

- The deeper you allow God to work in you, the wider, further and higher He can work through you. Whatever it takes, do the hard internal work.

- The more you pursue God the more you'll experience a revelation of His holiness. The Lord God who makes us holy.

- Sometimes God will keep you from the fire. Other times God will make you fireproof and take you through the fire.

- Pray like nobody's listening; give like nobody's watching; love like nobody's counting.

🕊 Trust in His timing. Rely on His promises. Wait for His answers. Believe in His power. Rejoice in His goodness. Relax in His presence.

🕊 Many of your ideas are answers to your prayers.

- 🐦 God is never going to let you down. Don't worry about anything, but instead pray about everything.

- 🐦 God has things under control.

🕊 Sometimes God will do the best of things in the worst of times. Never give up.

🕊 If you don't know how to pray, pray the word. Don't know the answer? Read the word. Don't know what to say, speak the word.

🕊 God does not always work immediately, but He always works. Never give up; ask, seek, find.

🕊 It's already done in Jesus name.

- Suffering never leaves you where it finds you; you either become bitter or better.

- Faith is accepting, believing, proclaiming, confessing and decreeing the will of God over your situation until it is established.

- When we think, "it's too late." God says, "I still have a plan."

- God is great not just because nothing is too big. God is great because nothing is too small.

🕊 If you want God to do exceedingly, abundantly, more than all you could ask or imagine, then start trusting him now with all your unknowns.

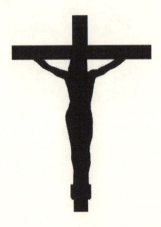

🕊 Worship will get you thru the roughest times in your life, because it shifts your focus from the problem to the problem solver.

- If you are going to enjoy your relationship with God, you must start spending time with Him.

- If you are feeling like God has forgotten you, ask Him to send you a sign that He hasn't.

🕊 You can choose to focus on your limitations or you can choose to embrace your unique God ordained purpose.

🕊 It is time; the world needs us now. Let us pull together in prayer for our earth and humankind, for all nations, and all living things.

🕊 It doesn't take a 20 minute prayer to get God's attention, some of your best prayers may just be three words: "Help me Lord."

🕊 Keep praying, even if you have only a whisper left.

- Don't let your worries keep you from worship. God is still worthy and still working on your behalf.

- Sometimes you don't get the strength out of prayer that you want. But you won't get any strength at all without prayer.

- Prayer is the heart beat of a believer.

- Don't bind yourself in chains that God has already freed you from. Your past mistakes have no power over His grace and forgiveness.

- Praying throughout the day allows you to have more peace.

- Meditating is like having a date with God.

🕊 Those who have not made God their all, will eventually make Him nothing. He's all or nothing.

🕊 You can't change people but you can pray for them, and that changes things.

🕊 We keep shouting our opinions; God keeps asking about our hearts.

🕊 Keep in mind: The tougher the lesson, the bigger the blessing.

🕊 Commit your works to the Lord and your plans will be established.

🕊 Say this: "Here I am Lord, send me."

🕊 Time with God is never time wasted, its time invested.

🕊 God is doing a new thing, not resurrecting the old thing.

- Discover God's truth for yourself.

- God can change your situation in an instant. Hang in there. Be of good courage.

🕊 Grace draws a circle around everyone and says they're in.

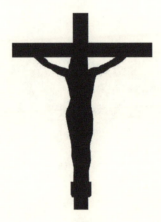

🕊 Worship is the strategy by which we interrupt our preoccupation with ourselves and attend to the presence of God.

🕊 Christianity is too rational for mysticism and too mystical for rationalism.

🕊 Sometimes to see even more clearly, you've got to close your eyes.

- If God brings you to it, he will bring you through it.

- Love your enemies and do good to those who hate you. Speak well of those who curse you.

🕊 Prayer can be simple, but it's not easy.

🕊 He will rescue you from the storm.

- Live in such a way that others see Jesus in you.

- People like to label you with everything you've done wrong, but you've already been labeled forgiven, redeemed, and restored.

🕊 Prayer is how the loves of our heart are re-ordered so we love God first and everything else second.

🕊 God is never too busy to listen. Don't be too busy to talk to Him.

- God's Word reminds us of His great love and kindness toward all who call upon Him.

- Take some time today to become very still, close your eyes, breathe deeply, and picture many angels surrounding you.

🕊 We should make the most of every opportunity to worship God.

🕊 Every time you see a blocked path, don't get upset. It could just be God's great guidance.

- In every hardship you have a choice - to pray and become a warrior, or to fret and become a worrier.

- Everything may be falling apart, but Jesus can piece you back together.

- That big hole in your life is a spiritual hole. No amount of wealth can ever fill it.

- God puts His strongest soldiers in the toughest battles.

🕊 When you pray, don't give God instructions.

🕊 God doesn't waste anything we go through. He knows how to bring good out of every situation.

- Sometimes we try to bury things, but the healing process begins when we let them come to light.

- God has put His wisdom and might on display for the world to see. He is worthy of our worship

🕊 If you can't find a way God will make one.

🕊 When we pray, we must believe that God, who is all-powerful, hears and acts on our behalf.

- It is amazing how God extends His blessings, grace, mercy. and love even when we don't deserve it.

- No need to worry, rush, doubt, or fear. God is always on time.

🕊 God doesn't care what you're not. He cares who you are. You are His. When He adds His extra to your ordinary, nothing is impossible for you.

🕊 God's mercies are new every morning. All you have to deal with today is today. Not yesterday, not tomorrow.

- God is the same yesterday, today, and forever.

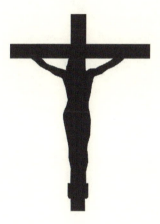

- Because of His mercy and grace, each day is an opportunity to do more with our God given talents and gifts.

- Satan attacks anyone God has chosen to promote. If you're under attack, God is getting ready to promote you.

- Ask God for wisdom and direction.

🕊 Becoming obsessed with what people think about you is the quickest way to forget what God thinks about you.

🕊 Sometimes God doesn't change your situation because he's trying to change your heart.

- Perseverance is not the result of our determination; it is the result of God's faithfulness.

- No God. No Peace. Know God. Know Peace.

🕊 When you recognize who Jesus is no one has to beg you to worship Him.

🕊 God does not number His army he calls His warriors by name.

🕊 Strengthen your faith.

🕊 The fear of the Lord is the root of a healthy, wise, powerful, secure life.

🕊 When God begins to do a new thing a new way the greatest opposition comes from the old thing with its old ways.

🕊 God cares about everything that concerns you, so feel free to talk to Him about anything.

🐦 Spending time with God is the key to our strength and success in all areas of life.

🐦 God believes in you; it's about time you do to.

🕊 Fasting increases both our capacity and sensitivity to the Holy Spirit. It exchanges what we bring for what he bestows.

🕊 If you truly believe there's power in prayer you'll pray differently, constantly and boldly.

🕊 Let us pray for peace: peace in the world and in each of our hearts.

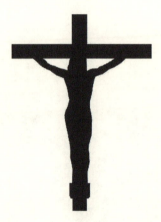

🕊 You have to stay passionate about what God put in your heart.

- 🕊 God will always bring the right people into your life, but you have to let the wrong people walk away.

- 🕊 God knows what we need when we need it. Trust that he knows how to put us at the right place at the right time.

🕊 Keep honoring God with your life, stay in peace, trust his timing, and God will open doors that no one can shut.

🕊 Kneeling to pray is often what gives you the strength to stand.

🕊 Satan knows your potential and his greatest fear is that you'll discover who you really are, what you're really worth and where you're headed.

🕊 When God gets ready to bless you he doesn't send complainers into your life. He sends people of faith and encouragement.

- When God opens the next door for you, walk through it with confidence in Him: knowing that it is indeed and in fact, your time.

- God is bigger than we think and greater than we think. Nothing is beyond His ability.

PART THREE
STAY HUMBLE

"Let your light shine forth before men that they may see your good works & give glory to your Father who is in heaven."

– Matthew 5:16

🕊 The Lord's Harvest is full of opportunities and introductions that will take you to new levels you didn't know exist.

🕊 When you have nothing but God, you discover that God is enough.

🐦 God gives grace to the humble.

🐦 May we always say thank you to God, especially for his patience and mercy.

- Stay humble in the sight of the Lord.

- There is never a reason to lose hope. Jesus says: "I am with you until the end of the world".

- Allow God to transform you from the inside out.

- The world tells us to seek success, power and money; God tells us to seek humility, service and love.

🕊 Sinner by nature. Saved by grace.

🕊 When you have a deep awareness of God, you are fully capable and prepared to deal with whatever life brings your way.

- Fear-based repentance makes us hate ourselves. Joy-based repentance makes us hate the sin.

- If we think we are not all that bad, the idea of grace will never change us.

- God will repair the shattered pieces of hope, and heal the broken pieces of your heart.

- Only God can change people.

🐦 God doesn't just restore broken lives. He makes them completely new.

🐦 It's during the struggle that you find out who you really are.

- Just me struggling to be true to who I am before God.

- Your faith is not tested by God, it's challenged by your ego.

🐦 Be grateful for small things, big things, and everything in between.

🐦 Count your blessings, not your problems.

- Holiness doesn't mean doing extraordinary things, but doing ordinary things with love and faith.

- Sin is not simply doing bad things, it is putting good things in the place of God.

- Christians need the gospel as much as non-Christians do.

- Believe in yourself, for you are a child of God.

🐦 Rather than focusing your attention on all that you need, discipline yourself to thank God for all that you have.

🐦 Give thanks for unknown blessings already on their way.

🕊 Generosity has an attitude, and it's called gratitude.

🕊 We are much better at noticing the works of someone else's sinful nature than we are at battling our own.

🐦 God's goodness transcends circumstances.

🐦 Love one another as Christ loved you.

🕊 Sometimes God's answers don't look like what we had in mind.

🕊 Thanksgiving should be our natural response to the goodness and Grace of God.

- 🕊 Even on your worst day, you are still sons and daughters of the king.

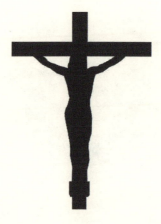

- 🕊 Love is always a demonstration; not just a set of words or a feeling.

- God's love and acceptance is enough, nothing else will be.

- Learn to lean on God's grace.

- Imagine how different the world would look if we prayed for people instead of judging them.

- Don't be too busy to notice what God is doing around you.

🕊 Sometimes man's rejection is God's protection.

🕊 Hearing God's word does not make one wise; but acting and responding on God's word makes one wise.

- Jesus went and interacted with people beyond his own.

- Christ restored us back to factory settings.

- The blessings of God in your life are not to be hoarded but to be shared.

- Trouble starts when you stop embracing God.

- Be a blessing to others.

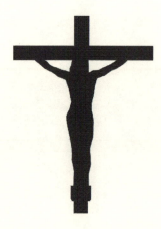

- If you truly have a relationship with God, Don't let Sunday be the only day of the week you talk to Him.

🐦 If eternity defines our existence, then morality must define our actions.

🐦 God has purpose for your pain, a motive for your struggle and a reward for your faithfulness.

- Humility is the surest sign of true strength.

- Worship is a way of life, not just a bunch of songs we sing on Sunday.

- Sometimes, the only thing you can do for someone is pray for them.

- BIG NEWS: God is good. Opening doors. One at a time.

- May our words be kinds and our hearts pure.

- Crisis is the opportunity to step out from among the ordinary, the mundane, the usual and embrace our destiny.

🐦 Only the word you act on will yield fruit.

🐦 Only what is sown gets multiplied.

🕊 The calling before you is greater than the calamity behind you.

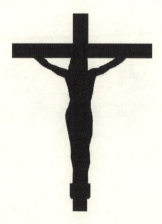

🕊 The results of your generosity will be visible.

- Keep learning and keep growing.

- The Lord reigns, Let the earth rejoice.

🕊 Encourage someone.

🕊 Take time to care.

🕊 Jesus makes life make sense.

🕊 Love is the measure of faith.

- 🕊 You cannot out give God.

- 🕊 All of life finds it's meaning in GOD and His love.

- Our greatest challenge is not our discipline or our devotion. Our greatest challenge is believing the Gospel.

- Hold on to grace tighter than you hold on to grudges.

- 🕊 No matter what happens during the night, God will still be there in the morning.

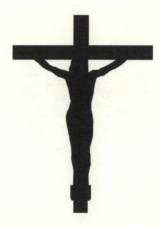

- 🕊 When things don't turn out how you expected, trust that God sees the big picture and is working every detail out for your good and his glory.

🐦 Fear God and you need not fear anything else or anyone else.

🐦 We are often caught up with our whole future. Let's trust God right now, and just take the next step.

🕊 To him who receives the revelation falls the responsibility.

🕊 God is more concerned about your heart than your performance. If your heart is right, your performance will eventually catch up.

🐦 You are fearfully and wonderfully made.

🐦 Maybe the most powerful words ever put together; God loves you.

🐦 God will give you strength for every battle, wisdom for every decision, peace that surpasses understanding.

🐦 If you don't enjoy what you have, how could you be happier with more? Be grateful God has blessed you.

🐦 Remember to divert daily, withdraw weekly and abandon annually to spend time with Jesus.

🐦 What you focus on, you magnify; the problem, or the solution. Trust God.

🕊 Without Jesus we can't bear fruit, but in and with him we can bear fruit.

🕊 Live so that others will want to know Christ.

- Don't say God is silent, when your Bible is closed.

- Pride builds walls; humility builds bridges.

- Lord cleanse me of anything that breaks your heart.

- It doesn't matter what you've done God still loves you.

🕊 Have faith in the power of prayers.

🕊 Look for God, He is not far.

- 🐦 Where God's will is already known, stop waiting and start declaring life.

- 🐦 God faithfully provides the strength we need to face the challenges of each new day.

🕊 We belong to God. He is our strong defense.

🕊 Dear God, please help me to clearly and confidently know the best path for me to take.

🕊 When you let yourself live beautifully, you're a portrait of heaven on Earth, and you inspire others with your joy and success.

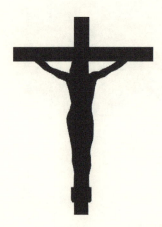

🕊 Blessings are all around us. Gratitude should be easy. Gratitude is the antidote for entitlement and it's arrogance.

🕊 Go to the Lord just as you are.

🕊 When things don't go the way you planned, thank God. It just means He has something better for you.

🕊 We all fall short, but God's grace never does.

🕊 Say this and believe it: "It is well with my soul."

- Following Jesus is sometimes going to put us on collision course with the status quo.

- The Holy Spirit gives us wisdom and boldness.

🐦 We don't need to make our light brighter we just need to take our light where it is darker.

🐦 If God can raise the dead, He can raise your chin. Lay down the shame, lift up your eyes, and follow the Lamb who has made you clean.

🐦 Thank-you God. Your Blessings are so rich and abundant that our hearts are overflowing with gratitude.

🐦 Emerge yourself into the presence of God through praise and worship I promise all your worries, doubts, and fears will vanish.

- As long as God is on the throne, there is always hope... it's not over.

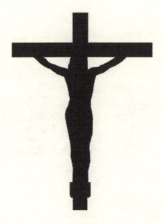

- God will open doors that no man can shut.

- Walk with God and every round will go higher.

- There is no sin that God cannot pardon. All we need to do is ask for forgiveness.

- Give Christ first priority in your life and watch everything else fall in line.

- God is able to do just what He said He would do.

- 🕊 For every one person that doubts you, God will send more people to believe in you.

- 🕊 You must live expecting to be blessed by God.

- Never let the presence of a storm cause you to doubt the presence of God.

- God can't and won't stop loving you. His love absolutely cannot be altered; it's constant.

🕊 Until you embrace your weakness you won't fully appreciate God's strength.

🕊 Lord, grant us the grace to know we are sinners.

🕊 Repentance is the most liberating word in the Bible. It frees us from guilt and it challenges us for greater things ahead.

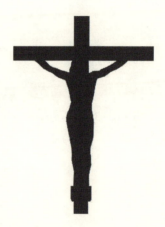

🕊 One of the greatest gifts you can give someone is to acknowledge and affirm God's gift on their life.

- 🐦 Content people don't always have the best of everything, but they make the best of everything.

- 🐦 If you are not ready to be criticized for your obedience to God, you are not ready to be used by God.

🕊 It all has a purpose: Every struggle, every victory and tiny detail in your life matters.

🕊 God is the strength of your life; it doesn't matter what may come your way.

- When you do what God wants you to do, He rewards you.

- Covenant will keep you connected even when offense tries to run you away.

- God is still in the miracle working business.

- Think about things of Heaven, not things of earth.

🕊 GOD's biggest blessings are hidden in Obedience.

🕊 GOD will move everything around in your life until your only option is to trust Him.

- God has been amazing.

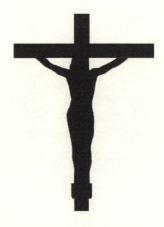

- Pain is real, but so is hope; hope in Jesus Christ. He is our very present help in the time of need.

🕊 Be a blessing and you will be blessed.

🕊 Life is so much better when you are grateful for what you have.

- 🐦 The challenges and difficulties we face are not engineered by God to hurt us.

- 🐦 Don't allow a spirit of fear to corrupt your ability to attract all the Holy Spirit has for you.

- God needs you to be an agent of healing and to forgive people you do not believe deserve forgiveness.

- Trust in God and He can restore your passion and help you discover new found motivation.

🐦 We have to come to a place where we are convinced that God is for us and not against us.

🐦 Life becomes peaceful and amazing when we begin to walk by faith and not by sight.

- When you sacrifice something for God, He always replaces it with something much better.

- Even if you are vile or lack virtue, God can fix it.

- Do not rely on your own strength. It will fail you when you need it most.

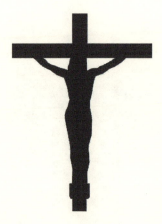

- When we open our hearts to his perfect love, we are touched by the Master's hand, and we are transformed.

- Learn to trust God, even when things are not going your way.

- God isn't wowed by fancy words; He delights in humble hearts.

- 🐦 God will always make a way out of no way.

- 🐦 Humility saves man: pride makes him lose his way.

🕊 You may be weak but God is strong.

🕊 Just because you don't see anything doesn't mean God isn't doing something.

- 🐦 It is when we suffer that we discover what we are really trusting and hoping in: ourselves, or God.

- 🐦 Even in our dark times, God is still there.

- The depth you're willing to allow God to take you is in direct proportion to the height He will elevate you.

- Every day wake up and thank God for everything in your life.

🐦 Your home is in Heaven; you are just traveling through this world.

🐦 Just know that God is faithful even when we are not.

- God's perfect plan for your life is not dependent on you being perfect. He is not surprised by your mistakes or moved by your circumstances.

- The gospel never gets old.

PART FOUR

SOAR HIGH WITH FAITH AND TRUST

"This I declare of the Lord:

He alone is my refuge, my place of safety;

he is my God, and I am trusting him."

– Psalm 91:2

🕊 God works in mysterious ways.

🕊 Faith sees the invisible, believes the incredible, and receives the impossible.

🕊 Only repeat what God says, besides, the devil says nothing worth repeating anyway.

🕊 Faith without action is dead.

- Your past is locked up tight. Future doors await you; enter into a season of grace and new beginnings.

- Sometimes God takes away something you never expected losing, but He will replace it with something you never imagined you could have.

- You can't have peace when you're at war with God.

- Too often we don't realize how great we have it until something is taken away. Don't take for granted what God has given you.

🕊 Keep honoring God with your life, stay in peace, trust His timing, and God will open doors that no one can shut.

🕊 Forgive so you can be free. Don't let the person who hurt you keep you in prison. Let God settle the score.

- 🕊 Don't allow the gifts He's given you to sit dormant...God has equipped each and every one of us for greatness.

- 🕊 God empowers you to remove people out of your life who are a detriment to your destiny.

🕊 Whatever you decree by faith, according to the will of God, must come to pass. Pray His word, stand in faith and prepare for His promises.

🕊 Walk boldly through the doors God opens for you, and don't become discouraged when He closes one.

- God is able through His mighty power at work within us, to accomplish infinitely more than we might ask or think.

- There is a season for weeping and a season for rejoicing.

- Remember, with Jesus there is always rebirth.

- Stop focusing on what's wrong with everyone else and start focusing on how blessed you are.

- Faith in God includes faith in His guidance.

- God provides a security that the world can never provide.

- Make sure becoming a Christian is not just a status update. You have to put the heart and work in to be a true Christian.

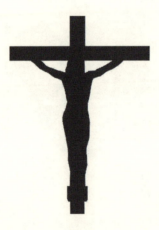

- Until God opens the next door, praise Him in the hallway.

- 🕊 God won't try to speak over all of the noise in our lives. Be still.

- 🕊 God finds us in the holes we dig for ourselves. Where we see failures; He sees foundations.

- Sometimes God leads us into failure so we'll experience more of His grace, not less of His love.

- Darkness wants us to live our lives worn out. Rest is holy.

- 🐦 Expect more from God and less from people. Only God can be God and people can only be people.

- 🐦 Don't demand from people what only God can give you. He is your source and wellspring for life.

- If God called you to something don't look around for approval from others, only listen to Him; it's your journey and chances are they won't even understand.

- Change comes by seeing a need for a Savior and getting one.

- Faith is not denying a problem exists; Faith is denying that it has position and control over your destiny.

- Faith in God means believing and trusting him based on who He is.

🕊 Faith in God means trusting Him without knowing how He will choose to handle it.

🕊 You don't have to figure out how to act like a Christian or how to break bad habits. Just get to know Jesus. He is life. The power is in Him.

- Everything God promised you, every dream He has placed on the inside, He still has every intention of bringing it to pass.

- If the Bible never challenges your assumptions, it's possible you aren't really hearing it.

🐦 You don't have to prove that God is doing a new thing in you. Keep living and let it spring forth. It will speak on your behalf.

🐦 Smile, things are working out. You may not see it now, but just know God is directing you to a much greater happiness.

- God loves all people equally.

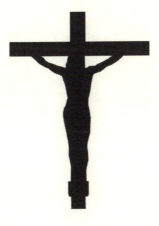

- God has an assignment with your name on it.

🐦 God is preparing you for greater things.

🐦 God can promote you to places that no one else can ever put you.

- It doesn't matter your background you qualify to be used by God.

- God wants to bless you in a way you're not expecting. Don't limit Him with your expectations.

🕊 Don't run ahead of God. Let him direct your steps He has plans. He has time. God's clock is never early or late. It always strikes on time.

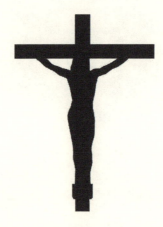

🕊 God is interested in you. He bothers to count the hairs on your head. You are valuable.

- The more we experience success, the more we have to keep surrendering it back to the Lord. Every good and perfect gift comes from above.

- Stop delegating to God things He has already given you power to do.

- Regardless of whatever you are going through, one thing is for sure; God is for you.

- Action without God's instruction and word is not faith but one's own doing.

🕊 Obedience turns faith into power.

🕊 Keep God's word in your heart and He'll keep your feet on the right path.

🕊 Success is not what you experience through ignoring Jesus. It's what you experience through exploring Jesus.

🕊 Show God your faith and He will show you His faithfulness.

🕊 God isn't looking for you to be perfect, but He does want you to be faithful. He doesn't require you to succeed, but He does ask you to try.

🕊 Faith is the key.

- You show how strong you are when times are tough. Stay the course. Trust in God. He will never lead you astray.

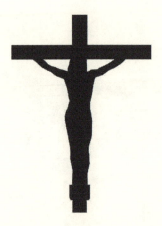

- God is able to do exceeding abundantly above all that we ask or think according to the power that work in us.

🐦 God's plan for you is always better for us than the plans we have for ourselves.

🐦 God heard you. Just be patient.

🕊 If you want to succeed in life and enjoy the blessings of God, you must intend to succeed. It won't happen by accident.

🕊 Faith is our positive response to what God has done by His grace. Its activated by His word.

- Fear not, for God is with you.

- Hope isn't all the things we're wishing for; it's all the things God's turning us into.

🕊 Grace is the free, unmerited favor of God, working powerfully on the mind and heart to change lives.

🕊 Fasting renews spiritual vision and faith.

🕊 When the joy of the Lord is your strength, circumstances and hardships lose their power to control your happiness.

🕊 Faith is praising God through the storm.

- 🕊 God's favor goes before you. His grace covers you from behind. You can't out run His love. You can never escape His goodness.

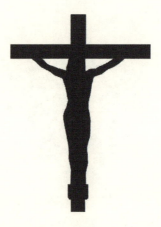

- 🕊 Remember Your Story. See how far the Lord has brought you.

🐦 Jesus, let me see people through your eyes.

🐦 God's unfailing love for you will not be shaken.

- 🕊 The power of His love breaks every chain.

- 🕊 God can bring peace to your past, purpose to your present, and hope to your future.

🕊 God's word has healing power.

🕊 God > My fears. God > My insecurities. God > My worry. God > My everything.

- God is working in your life right now in ways you cannot understand.

- Throw yourselves into the work of the Master, confident that nothing you do for Him is a waste of time.

- Don't settle for the mundane, the usual, or the common. You are extraordinary.

- Not a day goes by without God's grace unfolding in your life.

🐦 The strongest people aren't always the people who win, but the people who don't give up when they lose.

🐦 Christians sit in the midst of this world's sorrows tasting the coming joy.

- Your past does not exist to God. Jesus blood has cleansed you. It's gone so forget it.

- Every knee will bow and every tongue will confess, Jesus Christ is Lord.

- 🕊 But without faith it is impossible to please Him.

- 🕊 Have faith that everything will work out for the best.

- Knowing God is, knowing one person who will never give up on you.

- You are God's child; never forget that.

- 🕊 Though your heart is torn, praise God through the storm.

- 🕊 Never doubt that God has gotten you though every hard moment in your life.

🕊 God's "no" is not a rejection, it's a redirection.

🕊 You can't believe God's word and be in fear. Fear indicates you don't believe. Eliminate fear with faith and belief.

🐦 Man says show me and I'll trust you. God says trust me and I'll show you.

🐦 Cherish those you have in your life, because you never know when God will need them back.

🕊 Sometimes God Has To Break You Down To Bless You Up.

🕊 You can't get to where you're going without seasons of struggle. The valley prepares you for the mountaintop.

🕊 You are never alone, and the angels accompany you constantly, even when you are unaware of their presence.

🕊 You will never be alone as long as you have Jesus.

- No matter where we are in life, God has more in storm.

- God puts people in your life for a reason, and removes them from your life for a better reason.

- Don't give up on what God has called you to do.

- Worry does nothing but steal your joy and keep you very busy doing nothing.

- Faith is not belief without proof, but trust without reservation.

- Focus on God He is the solution.

- Don't make the mistake of trying to fight a spiritual battle with your human reasoning. Use the word of God and strike sure

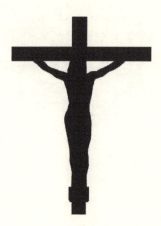

- He will catch you when you fall.

- 🕊 Your job is to take care of the possible and let God handle the impossible.

- 🕊 Sometimes, all it takes is just one prayer to change everything.

- God never leads us where He cannot keep us. His grace is always sufficient for us in any and every circumstance of life.

- God never shuts one door without opening another.

🕊 Pray, forgive yourself and appreciate others.

🕊 Don't be disappointed when people can't do for you what only God can. They are not your answer. God is.

🐦 No matter how things look, know that God is still in control. Stay in peace, knowing that He will always be with you.

🐦 God gave us talents because He wants us to use them.

🕊 Be humble in victory. Give God all the glory.

🕊 Hear what others have to say, but listen to God.

- 🐦 God cares about everything that concerns you.

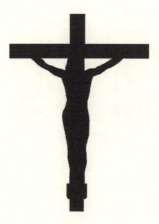

- 🐦 God hasn't changed His mind about you or filed your situation in a folder of lost causes.

- You don't have to have it all together for God to use you. He works through ordinary people with willing hearts and a teachable spirit.

- Show gratitude because you can't be blessed and stressed at the same time.

🐦 Having faith does not mean having no difficulties, but having the strength to face them, knowing we are not alone.

🐦 Your praise to God forces you to minimize trouble and maximize God.

- No matter what you are facing today, praise Him right where you are.

- Always do good unto others, God will surely send others to do good unto you.

- God is Full of Grace for disgraceful people.

- Look back and thank God.
  Look forward and trust God.
  Look around and serve God.
  Look inside and find God.

🕊 The God you serve is bigger than the problems you encounter.

🕊 Ordinary becomes extraordinary when we apply God's word to everyday life.

- The renewing of our minds is a process of believing more of what The Father says about us, than our wounds do.

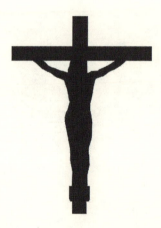

- Even when life is confusing and tough, the faithfulness of God remains true. Don't let go, God never will.

- Encouragement is water to a thirsty soul, nourishment to a hungry heart, peace to a weary spirit and life to a dying hope.

- Tell Jesus you're desperate for awakening. Ask Him to give you eyes to see, ears to hear. Ask Him to make His words like fire in your bones.

🐦 If you have faith but never take a step, you'll never reach your God-given destiny. Be bold, step out and watch your dreams become a reality.

🐦 God is bigger than your history and passionate about your destiny.

🐦 God who carried you yesterday won't drop you today.

🐦 Stay strong. Your test will become your testimony, and your mess will become your message.

🕊 Faith doesn't make things easy it makes them possible.

🕊 No matter what tomorrow holds, we can rest easy knowing that God holds every moment in His hands, good and bad.

🕊 Let go of fear and trust God.

🕊 Grace finds goodness in everything.

- 🕊 Knock and the door will be opened to you.

- 🕊 Pray to have eyes that see the best, a heart that forgives the worst, a mind that forgets the bad, and a soul that never loses faith.

- It's easy to quit, but it takes faith to go through.

- God can turn around any situation.

🕊 Put on the full armor of God.

🕊 Let us allow God to fill our hearts with His goodness and mercy.

🕊 Ministry isn't a day job; it's a lifestyle.

🕊 Without dreams, we reach nothing. Without love, we feel nothing. And without God, we are nothing.

- In the roughest moments, remember: God is our Father; God does not abandon His children.

- With God, all things are possible.

🕊 God + nothing = everything
Everything – God = nothing

"But the fruit of the Spirit is love, joy, peace, patience, kindness, goodness, faithfulness.5"
– Galatians 5:22

"But prove yourselves doers of the word, and not merely hearers who delude themselves."

– James 1:22

"Be strong and of good courage. Don't be afraid."
- Deuteronomy 31:6

"Let the words of my mouth and the meditation of my heart be acceptable in your sight, O LORD, my rock and my redeemer."
- Psalms 19:14

AFTER THOUGHTS FROM THE AUTHOR

It's never too late to be what you could have been. Start today adjusting your attitude and outlook, and your results for ensuring a productive lifestyle will be made more effectively. Wherever you are in your life, let *THE HOPE HANDBOOK* guide you in a new direction to a new start, in helping you realize how much control you have over your own life.

Always remember, we create the hope or the fear in our lives by the thoughts and ideas we put into action.

ABOUT THE AUTHOR

With more than a decade of experience, **Germany Kent**, also known as The Hope Guru™, has enjoyed a successful consulting business with clients from all walks of life. Germany is a dynamic public speaker. She has been awarded multiple times for speaking.

She has appeared nationally on The Drs, The Food Network, NBC, CBS, ABC, Disney, MTV, and BET, just to name a few.

She was previously listed in Who's Who Among Young Americans.

As Germany's brand has grown, both domestic and internationally, she has picked up more than a few fans who remain interested in her status. This has catapulted her into a category of respected power and influence, especially on social media, where she has been cited as a top social media influencer.

Germany is dedicated and committed to giving back to the community. She is dedicated to helping others reach their highest potential. She engages herself as a coach and mentor, another platform that Germany is immensely committed too.

Germany graduated with honors from The University of Alabama and Mississippi State University. She resides in Southern California where she is an entertainment host and successful commercial actress. As a media personality, Germany has interviewed power players, newsmakers and Hollywood royalty. She has landed interviews with Oscar, Emmy, Golden Globe, and Grammy-award winning performers.

Germany offers messages of HOPE on Twitter and continues to be a social media magnet.

You can follow her @germanykent to receive her messages of motivation and inspiration onto your timeline.

TO OUR READERS

Star Stone Press, publishes books on topics ranging from spirituality, personal growth and self-help to inspiration, technology, family, and social titles. Our mission is to publish quality books that will contribute to the wellbeing of the reader.

Our readers are our most important resource, and we value your input and ideas. Please feel free to contact us.

Mail to:

Star Stone Press
10736 Jefferson Blvd #164
Culver City, CA 90230

Message From Germany
If you have enjoyed my book, please consider writing and posting a customer review at Amazon.com, Goodreads.com and/or LibraryThing.com. I would really appreciate your support.

Visit Germany on the web at:
www.TheHopeGuru.com

Made in the USA
Monee, IL
13 December 2021